The Don't Laugh Challenge

Easter Edition

FREE DOWNLOADS

For your FREE Coloring Pages
Visit us at:

http://www.wordofmm.com/

YOUR DOWNLOAD CODE:

JOKES1

The Don't Laugh Challenge Instructions:

- Sit down facing your opponent at eye level.

- Take turns reading jokes to each other.

- First person to make the opponent laugh, wins a point!

- First person to 3 points wins & is crowned The Don't Laugh MASTER.

Game on!

EASTER
JOKES

1.   Who hides inside an egg?

Someone who's a little chicken.

2.   What kind of egg can't make it's mind up?

An omelette you know.

3.   Why did the Easter Bunny have to leave school?

He was eggspelled.

4.   What does Jesus and dough have in common?

You celebrate when they rise.

5.   What's the most annoying kind of a egg?

A practical yolker.

6. Why can't scrambled eggs win races?

Because they're always beaten.

7. What do you say if you throw an egg at someone?

The yolks on you.

8. Why was the Easter bunny wearing a hat?

He was having a bad hare day.

9. How did the pirate Easter Bunny find his treasure?

Eggs marked the spot.

10. What did the Easter Bunny say to the carrot on a date?

I'd like to get to gnaw you.

11. Why do soft boiled eggs always catch hard boiled eggs?

They're better at running.

12. What happened when the Easter egg heard a funny joke?

It cracked up

13. Why did the Easter Bunny join the library?

Because he loves to burrow things.

14. Why did the Easter bunny throw eggs at his friend?

He wanted to egg him on.

15. Why should you crack your Easter eggs into a pan on Friday?

Because it's a good fry day.

16. Why did the Easter Bunny go jogging?

He was getting his eggcercise.

17. What kind of jewelry does the Easter Bunny?

Anything so long as it has lots of karats

18. Why is there trouble around the Easter Bunny?

Because it's always a harey situation.

19. How did the doctor examine the Easter Bunny?

With an Eggs ray.

20. How did the Easter Bunny gamble?

With lucky rabbits feet.

21. How can you tell if it's really the Easter Bunny?

Ask him to tell a joke and see if it's bunny.

22. Why did the woman rub the Easter Bunny on her head after the shower?

She thought he was a Hare dryer.

23. What do you call an Easter bunny with fleas?

Bugs bunny

24. What kind of Easter egg travels down the Amazon?

An Eggsplorer.

25. Why is the Easter Bunny religious?

Because he always Hops and prays.

26. Why did the Easter eggs strike?

They were being eggsploited.

27. What hops and foams at the mouth?

A rabid rabbit.

28. What kind of eggs does a dog get at Easter?

Pooched eggs.

29. What is the Easter Bunny's Olympic sport?

Hop scotch.

30. Who's going to play the Easter Bunny in movies?

Rabbit De Niro

31. Don't make an anagram of Easter.

It'll only end in tears.

32. What do you call a yellow bunny?

The Easter Bun-nana

33. How does the Easter Bunny fly?

By hare plane

34. What do you sing to the Easter Bunny once a year?

Hoppy birthday

35. Why are egg white omelettes serious?

They're no yolk

36. Why was the egg yolk shy?

He didn't want to come out of his shell.

37. How does the Easter Bunny get rid of termites?

Eggs-terminates them!

38. Why did the egg go to the party dressed as a cod?

He was being shell fish.

39. How do you spy on the Easter Bunny?

Bug bunny

40. What's the Easter bunnies second favorite vegetable after carrots?

Egg plants

41. Where does the Easter Bunny buy pancakes?

At the IHOP.

42. What happens to the Easter Bunny when Easter is over?

He lives Hoppily ever after.

HAPPY EASTER!

Q&A

150

QUESTION & ANSWER

JOKES

1. What made the beet turn red?

   He saw the salad dressing

2. Why do pirates like to sing?

   To hit the high C's

3. What's the cats favorite singer?

   Kitty Perry

4. Who won the pencil fight?

   No one, it was a draw

5 What's the best way to catch a fish?

A pick up line

6. What flower is the best kisser?

Tulips

7. Why are fish easy to weigh?

They have their own scales

8. What is the math teacher's favorite dessert?

Pi

9. Why don't ghost drink?

They can't handle their boos

10. What happened to the soap addict?

He got clean

11. Why did the man get fired from the calendar store?

He took a day off

12. What award does dentist of the year get?

A little plaque

13. Why did the baker go broke?

He didn't make enough dough

14. Why did the banker quit his job?

He lost interest

15. What did the beaver say to the log?

Nice gnawing you

16. What did the hat say to the shoes?

You stay here, I'll go on a head

17. Why was the teacher cross-eyed?

She couldn't control her pupils

18. Why shouldn't you fart at the Apple Store?

They don't have Windows

19. Why wasn't the builder successful?

He didn't do his homework

20. Why are fish so clever?

They're always in schools

21. Why wouldn't Bruce Wayne pitch at baseball?

Because he always preferred to bat.

22. What tablet do frogs use?

The Lilly-pad

23. What animal loves playing the saxophone?

A bluesbird

24. Why can't you teach Cowboys Art?

Because if you ask them to draw they will shoot you

25. What kind of pasta do zombies eat at school?

100% whole brain

26. What dogs can go to church?

Saint Bernards

27. What kind of socks do pirates wear?

Arrrggile

28. Have you ever seen a catfish?

No, how would he hold the pole?

29. What do dogs wear when they are tired?

Pants

30. Where does water go to relax?

Gulf course

31. Why did the pigs leave the party?

It was a boar

32. Why did the boy put peanut butter in the printer?

To go with the paper jam

33. What is the best horn for the bathroom?

Tuba toothpaste

34. Why are bananas so attractive?

A peel

35. How do you make fruit punch?

Make it mad

36. Why did the horse go to the wedding?

She needed a groom

37. Why did the grasshopper stop drinking coffee?

He was too jumpy

38. What did the carpet say to the floor?

I've got you covered

39. What's a cat's favorite color?

Purr-ple

40. Why did the taco go to the dentist?

He lost his filling

41. Where do polar bears go to dance?

Snowballs

42. What do baseball players eat on?

Home plates

43. What cat can't go to the casino?

A cheetah

44. What days start with T?

Today and Tomorrow

45. What kind of table can you eat?

Vegetable

46. What do cows do at night?

Look at the moooooooon

47. What snakes are good at math?

Adders

48. How do you make a jellyfish laugh?

Ten-Tickles

49. What do you call rabbits walking backwards?

A receding hare line.

50. What's a boxer's favorite drink?

Punch

51. Why aren't needles flat?

There is no point

52. Why did the pilot change his pants?

He was in a no-fly zone

53. Why doesn't corduroy make good pillows?

They make headlines

54. Why did the fish go to medical school?

To become a sturgeon

55. What do you do when you become addicted to twitter ?

Get Tweetment

56. Why were the marionettes for sale so cheap?

No strings attached

57. Why can't dogs go shopping?

They can't find a barking spot

58. When is the best time to get a tan?

Sunday

59. What's the best way to learn braille?

Get a feel for it

60. How do rabbits travel?

By hareplane

61. Why was the birthday cake sad?

It was in tiers

62. Did you hear the one about the German sausage?

It was the wurst

63. Why did the boat sale have extra paddles?

It was an oar deal

64. How did the new chef get his job?

He made the cut

65. Why was it so hot at the concert?

The fans left

66. What's the smartest bug?

A spelling bee

67. Where do fish look for jobs?

The kelp-wanted board

68. What do you call a funny chicken?

A comedi-hen

69. How do you stop dogs chasing people on bicycles?

Take away their bikes.

70. Why did the cashew go to the hospital?

He was assaulted

71. What happens when you read in the sun?

You become well red

72. Did you hear about the new mop?

It's cleaning up

73. What kind of underpants do reporters wear?

News briefs

74. Why did the chicken cross the playground?

To get to the other slide

75. What kind of fish makes movies?

A starfish

76. What happened to the tired kangaroo?

He was out of bounds

77. When did the horse talk?

Whinny wanted to

78. What do you call a peanut on the moon?

An astro-nut

79. Why don't they serve candy in jail?

It makes you break out

80. Why did the man stand outside the donut shop?

They are worth the weight

81. What type of hair does the ocean have?

Wavy

82. What day do potatoes like?

Fryday

83. What did the cream say to the coffee?

I love you a latte

84. What is the best name for a lawyer?

Sue

85. Why did the lazy man open a bakery?

To loaf around

86. Why did the toast miss school?

He was feeling crumby

87. How can a dentist make you royalty?

By giving you a crown

88. What kind of underpants do clouds wear?

Thunderpants

89. What do you call a lamp on a diet?

Light eater

90. Why are tennis matches so loud?

They play with a raquet

91. What do you do with a broken shoe?

Let it heel

92. Where do you go when the Air conditioner breaks?

Fan Club

93. Why did the onion cry?

He cut himself

94. Why do traffic lights go red?

They have to change in front of people

95. What does grandpa throw in the winter?

Slow balls

96. Where do cats go on holiday?

The meow-seum

97. Did you hear about the kidnapping in the park?

He slept right through lunch

98. What do cows read?

Cattle logs

99. What the worst ice cream cone?

Pine

100.   Why was the banker sad?

He had no cents of humor

101. What did Sherlock Holmes investigate as a schoolboy?

His pencil case

102. Does an apple a day really keep the doctor away?

If you throw it at them hard enough.

103. What bow is always wet?

A rainbow

104. What's the most beautiful part of school?

The school-belle

105. Why did the baseball player get arrested?

He stole a base

106. Where do boxers get an education?

A school of fought

107. What do selfish people wear to school?

A me-niform.

108. What do you have to look at longest to understand?

The periodic table

109. When can you learn about car maintenance?

Brake time

110. Why was Spiderman bullied at school?

He was always crawling to teacher

111. Why did the handlebars fall off?

They saw the sign for 'bike sheds'

112. What kind of phones do they have in jail?

Cell phones

113. Why was coffee banned from the staff room?

Because of all the tea-chers

114. What can you play on a really hot day?

Hop-scorch

115. What's an Australian kids favourite candy?

W&W

116. In which class do you say "Gee...that's interesting..."?

G-ography

117. Why did the schoolboy's mouth taste of wood?

He had chips for lunch

118. Why was the schoolboy too hot in his uniform?

He was wearing a blazer

119. Why was the teacher so excited about world war two?

He was suffering from historya

120. Why do fish get paid more at the end of the school year?

They get a prom-ocean

121. What do cats sing along to?

Meowsic

122. Which animal loves dancing?

The discow

123. Which animal loves to feel things on your skin?

A mole

124. What insect can you catch with jelly?

A peanut butter fly

125. What bird is the biggest thief?

A robbin

126. Why do wolves like cards so much?

They hunt in packs

127. What bird can go fast in a rowboat?

The c-row

128. Why do cows never get parking tickets?

They always mooove

129. Where do baby cats sleep when they go camping?

In a kittent

130. Which animal likes to lick the pancake bowl?

The batterfly

131. How much milk do cows give their kids?

A calf pint

132. Which animal always keeps a hammer and screwdriver handy?

A turtool

133. Why are bees so successful in the army?

They always earn their stripes

134. Why are bees so famous?

There's always a buzz about them

135. Why did the pig learn karate?

So he could give a pork chop

136. What did the hippy tiger do?

Became a tie-dye-ger

137. Which animal makes the best secret agent?

A spy-der

138. How does a cat blend cake mix, or mix pancake batter?

It uses its whiskers

139. Why do bikes need a kickstand?

They are two tired

140. What happens when you eat too much Shawarma?

You falafel

141. Why did the portrait go to prison?

He got framed

142. What school did Sherlock Holmes go to?

Elementary Watson.

143. Why did the computer go to the hospital?

He had a bad virus

144. Which dog can understand morse code?

A dot dot dash-hund

145. What do you call a Frenchman who steps on a cat?

Clawed

146. What dog always lies?

A golden deciever

147. Where do cats do their tweeting?

In their twitter tray.

148. What's the shyest fish?

A koi carp.

149. How do you recognise an elephant's writing?

By it's elefont

150. How did the bird know it was good at tennis?

It was seeded

100
KNOCK- KNOCK
JOKES

1. Knock Knock
who's there?
Hanna
Hanna who?
Hanna me the key so I can open the door

2. Knock Knock
who's there?
owls go...
owls go who?
Man you are smart.

3. Knock Knock
who's there?
Wanda
Wanda who
Wanda go somewhere and have some fun?

4. Knock knock
Who's there?
Who who
who-who-who?
Santa is that you?

5. Knock knock
Who's there?
Yah
Yah who?
Settle down, cowboy!

6. Knock knock
Who's there?
Reed
Reed who?
Redo it? Ok knock knock

7. Knock knock
Who's there?
Contin
Contin who?
That's it, just Contin

8. Knock Knock
Who's there?
Snow
Snow who?
Snow one you know

9. Knock Knock
Who's there?
Owls Say
Owls Say who?
Good, now what does a cow say?

10. Knock Knock
Who's there?
Anita
Anita who
Anita get a new key!

11. Knock Knock
Who's there?
Dwayne
Dwayne who?
Dwayne is coming down hard, open up!

12. Knock Knock
Who's there?
Butch
Butch who?
Butch your eye on the keyhole and you'll see

13. Knock Knock
Who's there?
Value
Value who?
Value you just open the door?

14. Knock Knock
Who's there?
Irish
Irish who?
Irish you would let me in.

15. Knock Knock
Who's there?
Noah
Noah who?
Noah garage near here? My car broke down.

16. Knock Knock
Who's there?
Hanna
Hanna who?
Hanna hard time finding my key

17. Knock Knock
Who's there?
Cushion
Cushion Who?
Cushion just let me in.

18. Knock Knock
Who's there?
Casey
Casey who?
Casey you're hungry, I brought lunch

19. Knock Knock
Who's there
Roach
Roach who?
Roach you a note, told you I was coming.

20. Knock Knock
Who's there?
Isabel
Isabel who?
Isabel broken? I've been knocking for ten minutes

21. Knock Knock
Who's there?
Window
Window who?
Window we go to the movie?

22. Knock Knock
Who's there?
Goat
Goat who?
Goat get the key and let me in!

23. Knock Knock
Who's there?
Ticket
Ticket who?
Ticket chance on me.

24. Knock Knock
Who's there?
Dozen
Dozen who?
Dozen my voice sound familiar?

25. Knock Knock
Who's there?
Ivana
Ivana who?
Ivana go to the park, want to come?

26. Knock Knock
Who's there?
Cold
Cold who?
Cold you lend me a dollar?

27. Knock Knock
Who's there?
Leaf
Leaf who?
Leaf the door unlocked

28. Knock Knock
Who's there?
Donut
Donut who?
Donut have my key.

29. Knock knock
Who's there?
Roof
Roof who?
Roof day, may I come in?

30. Knock Knock
Who's there?
Tommy
Tommy who?
Tommy you'll always be beautiful

31. Knock Knock
Who's there?
Shirley
Shirley who?
Surely you recognise me by now

32. Knock Knock
Who's there?
Autstralian Dan
Australian Dan who?
Down here, I'm very short!

33. Knock Knock
Who's there?
Mickey
Mickey who?
Me key's broken, let me in

34. Knock Knock
Who's there?
Paul
Paul who?
Paul the door open, it's cold out here!

35. Knock Knock
Who's there?
Terry
Terry who?
Terry-bull weather out here, open up!

36. Knock Knock. Who's there?
Woo.
Woo Who!
Are you having a party in there? It sounds fun!

37. Knock Knock.
Who's there?
I've got duffle
I've got duffle who?
Well don't give it to me I've just got over a cold

38. Knock Knock.
Who's there?
supercalifragilisticexpialidocious
Supercalifra- oh just come in

39. Knock Knock Knock Knock.
Who's there??
Why have you got 2 doors?

40. Knock Knock.
Who's there?
Ah.
Ah Who?
Cover your mouth when you sneeze!

41. Knock Knock.
Who's there?
Ophelia
Ophelia who?
Ophelia key under the carpet so I'll let myself in

42. Knock Knock.
Who's there?
Adjuster.
Adjuster Who?
Adjuster peephole & you'll be able to see

43. Knock Knock.
Who's there?
Assister
Assister who?
A sister of mine told me you were having a
party so let me in

44. Knock Knock.
Who's there?
Notra
Notra who?
No honestly I'm not lying

45. Knock Knock.
Who's there?
Easter
Easter who?
Easter be expected that you'd say that

46. Knock Knock.
Who's there?
Dejav
Dejav Who?
Knock Knock.

47. Kneck kneck
Who's there?
Two Giraffes

48. Knock Knock.
Who's there?
Blush!
Blush who?
I didn't even sneeze

49. Knock Knock.
Who's there?
Oscar
Oscar who?
Oscar if she can let me in it's freezing out here

50. Knock Knock.
Who's there?
I'm on Ya
I'm on ya Who?
I'm on yahoo too! Why don't you e mail me?

51. Knock Knock.
Who's there?
Marie
Marie who?
Ma reading glasses are broken so I can't see the bell

52. Knock Knock.
Who's there?
I'd
I'd Who?
I now pronounce you man & wife

53. Knock Knock.
Who's there?
Waster.
Waster who?
Waster time knocking if you don't even
remember me

54. Knock Knock.
Who's there?
Meat.
Meat Who.
Me three

55. Knock Knock.
Who's there?
New York.
New York Who?.
Knew your key wouldn't work that's why knocked

56. Knock knock
Who's there?
dood
dood who?
don't be disgusting, just let me in.

57. Knock knock
who's there?
Eskimo Igl
Eskimo Iglwho?
I thought it was cold!

58. Knock knock
Who's there?
Shamp
Shamp who?
I just washed my hair!

59. Knock knock
Who's there?
Bucker
Buckerwho?
Howdy cowboy!

60. Knock knock
Whos's there?
Tab
Tabwho?
Well if it's taboo we can't mention it.

61. Knock knock
Who's there?
Cook
Cookwho?
Is it spring already?

62. Knock knock
Who's there?
Water
Water who?
Has Napoleon returned!?

63. Knock knock
Who's there?
Tish
Tish who?
Are you going to sneeze?

64. Knock knock
Who's there?
Canned
Canned who?
That's the right attitude!

65. Knock knock
Who's there?
Pauline
Pauline who?
It's Pauline with rain let me in!

66. Knock knock
Who's there
Pill
Pill who?
Pillow fight!

67. Knock knock
Who's there?
Isit really?
Isit really who.
Yes who did you think it was?

68. Knock knock
Who's there?
Mell
Mell who?
Mellwho Yellhoo

69. Knock knock
Who's there?
Phil
Phil Who?
My fellow country men

70. Knock knock
Who's there?
Atole
Atole who?
Atole you to let me in!

71. Knock knock
Whos there?
Simon
Simon who?
Simon on the dotted line, I've got a package for you

72. Knock knock
Who's there?
Shhh
Shh who?
Well that's not very welcoming

73. Knock knock
Who's there?
Jill
Jill Who?
I go with every body! Don't understand

74. Knock knock
Who's there?
Hal
Hal Who?
Hallo, is it me you've been looking for.

75. Knock knock
Who's there?
Yaar
Yaar who?
Eek a werewolf!

76. Knock Knock
Who's there?
Comt
Comt who?
I don't know where you're going

79. Knock knock
Who's there?
Bell
Bell who?
No need to shout just let me in

80. Knock Knock
Who's there?
Keel
Keel who?
Nobody! Are you as assassin?!

81. Knock Knock
Who's there?
Ben
Ben who
Ben over and look through the keyhole,
you'll see who it is

82. Knock knock
Toodle
Toodle who?
But I just got here!

83. Knock Knock
Who's there?
Dijon
Dijon who?
Dijon want to dance?

84. Knock Knock
Who's there?
Hearty
Hearty who?
Hearty a day goes by I don't miss you.

85. Knock Knock
Who's there?
Nina Tent
Nina Tent who?
Let's play Mario!

86. Knock Knock
Who's there
Doris
Doris who?
Doris stuck, give it a push

87. Knock knock
who's there?
chell
chell who?
Are you here for the orchestra?

88. Knock Knock
Who's there?
Avenue
Avenue who?
Avenue got a peephole in the door?

89. Knock knock
who's there?
me
me who?
you should really know your name by now

90. Knock Knock
Who's there?
Boat
Boat who
Boat time you found out

91. Knock Knock
Who's there?
Neil
Neil who?
Neil down before me

92. Knock Knock
who's there?
sheep
sheep who?
sheep who are standing outside your door

93. Knock Knock
who's there?
Norton hears a..
Norton hears a who?
No, it's HORTON hears a who

94. Knock Knock
who's there?
who
who who
It's not polite to mimic

99. Knock Knock
who's there?
it's me, i've been standing right in front of you!

100. Knock Knock
who's there?
Yee
Yee who?
What are you so happy about?

50
RIDDLES

1. Why should you throw glasses into the Mississippi?
   It's got 4 eyes and it still can't see.

2. What begins with T, end with T and has T in it's middle?
   Tea pot.

3. Why didn't the sailor want to recite the alphabet?
   He was scared of being lost at c.

4. How many months have 28 days?
   All 12 of them

5. What do you lose if you share it even once?
   A secret.

6. Why are things always in the last place you look?
   Because when you find them you stop looking.

7. Why did the cowboy always ride into town on a Friday?
Friday was the name of his horse.

8. How far can you run into the woods?
Half way, then you're running out of it.

9. If you push my buttons, I'll take you for a ride,
you'll probably find it uplifting. What am I?
An elevator.

10. What joins two people but only touches one?
A wedding ring

11. Who shears the sheep?
The baaaaabaaaar

12. What did the cat say when the boy pulled his tail?
Mee-ow

13. What travels everywhere and never leaves the corner?
A stamp

14. What can you catch that is never thrown?
The flu

15. I did sleep for eight days. How did I do this?
I sleep at night

16. What did the cat say when he got a second dinner"
That too me-ouch

17. Mrs. Gardener is 5'8" tall. What does she weigh?
Vegetables

18. Janet's mom had 4 kids. She named the first one January, the second one February, the third one March, what did she name the forth one?
Janet. Jane't mom had 4 kids.

19. What was the biggest mountain before Mount Everest was discovered?
Mount Everest is still the biggest, even though it hadn't been discovered

20. Mike can always guess the score of any game before it starts. How can he do this?
The score before the game starts is 0-0

21. What has roads, but no cars, lakes but no fish, cities but no people?
A map

22. What has a 13 hearts but isn't alive?
A deck of card

23. What flies when it's new, is still for all it's life and runs when it does?
A snowflake

24. What keeps getting bigger the more you take from it?
A hole

25. A squirrel, a bird and a cat all race up the mango tree?
The winner gets the banana.
Who won?
There are no bananas on a mango tree

26. If you are rich, you need it. If you are poor, you have it. If
you eat it, you will die. What is it?
Nothing

27. What has teeth but can't eat?
A comb

28. I am made of water but I am not wet. What am I?
A cloud

29. The more you take, the more you leave behind.
What is it?
Footsteps

30. What joins two people but only touches one?
A wedding ring

31. I've got 4 legs and you can hop on my back, but we're going nowhere. What am I?
Table.

32. The more you cut me, the sharper I get, but it's easy to wear me down. What am I?
A pencil.

33. What is millions of years old but only a month old?
The moon

34. I have hands but I never clap. What am I?
A clock.

35. If I draw a line, how can I make it longer without adding anything to it?
Draw a shorter line next to it.

36. A girl rode her bike to her grandmother's house on Monday, stayed two days and rode home on Monday. How did she do it?
He bike is named Monday

37. Why did the greedy man have a calendar for dessert?
Because it was full of sundaes.

38. Why is it easy for cowboys to heard cats if there are no
other animals in the herd?
Because it's a cat-all herd.

39. How did the jockey win the race without a steed?
He just shouted till he was hoarse.

40. What has eyes but can't see?
Needles

41. What grows roots on top, lives in the cold
and dies in the heat?
An Icicle

42. What does a library and a chicken's dictionary got in
common?
They're both full of book, book.

43. What kind of bands do whales play in?
Orca-stra

44. What cheese is made backwards?
Edam

45. If everyone drove a white car, what would that be?
A white carnation

46. What allows you to look through a wall?
A window

47. Why is an island like the letter T?
They're both in the middle of water.

48. Why did the cows go to the city?
To see the mooseums

49. What room never has doors or windows?
A mushroom.

50. Why is it easy to cook eggs?
Because you always crack it.

50
TONGUE
TWISTERS

1. Big bald Billy brought bananas back from Bahamas

2. Kelly can't cook corn cobs camping in Canada

3. Eight eyed elves ate eleven eggs on Easter eve

4. Kitty quacked quick kisses and kicks on Christmas

5. Fuzzy flowers fear feathers for fat father's feet

6. Sick thin thorns threw six thick thongs

7. Crunchy crusts crumble crisp couches

8. Dark ducks draw dangling doodles of dragons on doors

9. Fifty fat frogs farted for fifteen funny foxes

10. Becky buys broken bonnets and bon bons

11. Little Lily likes licking long lollies along the lake

12. Sheep sneeze when cheese sees keys

13. Many monkeys make money mumbling marbles

14. Poopy puppies put prices past presents

15. Yellow yards yank yarn yonder

16. Purple pancakes put pouty people pint

17. Thirty thirsty thieves threw three thistles through Thursday

18. Patty put pennies in pretty pickle pies

19. Juggling jokers jump jaunty jingling jacks

20. Quick Queens quit cutting cute quilts

21. As snug as a bug stuck on a pug inside a rug

22. I shook the slumbering sheikh awake to shuttle him to the flight he'd take

23. The old clock on block went tick tock tock tick around the clock

24. The right knight fights for the right to fight for right althrough the night

25. Fred fed Ted bread, and Ted fed Fred bread

26. The big bug bit the little beetle bit the big bug back

27. Peter planted peppers in a perfect pepper plot

28. I petted a red pet in a pet bet with a vexed vet

29. I switched a swiss watch swiftly at the wrong cost

30. Peter picked a proper cup of coffee in a proper coffee cup

31. No need to light a night-light on a light night like tonight.

32. Two little lions lazing on a lino floor

33. My grand dad Stan got in a jam on the way to Afghanistan

34. Which witch watched which witch sew a switch

35. Roberta ran rings around the Roman ruins.

36. White rice is the nicest rice at the highest price

37. I don't know what a rhino knows about his nose

38. Extra quick Eddie edited it.

39. How many ants can ant eater eat, if an anteater wasn't quick on its anteater's feet?

40. How many tacks can a tax collector tax if a tax collector taxed taxes on tacks.

41. The teacher couldn't reach her on the bleachers beneath her

42. The coach got off the couch to get on the coach

43. I'm a very private principle but i'm far from invincible

44. A single segment of significance is sensible

45. I booked a cookbook for the bookmobiles book nook

46. The ghost lost the most hosts on the coast

47. I saw silly Sally sit upon a seat above a smooth pit

48. I emailed a female who couldn't receive my airmail

49. I like blueberries in a big bread pudding

50. We come in peace, please don't call the police

Made in the USA
Lexington, KY
26 March 2018